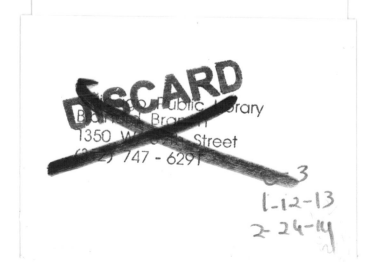

📖 READERS

Level 2

Dinosaur Dinners
Fire Fighter!
Bugs! Bugs! Bugs!
Slinky, Scaly Snakes!
Animal Hospital
The Little Ballerina
Munching, Crunching, Sniffing,
  and Snooping
The Secret Life of Trees
Winking, Blinking, Wiggling,
  and Waggling
Astronaut: Living in Space
Twisters

The Story of Pocahontas
Horse Show
Survivors: The Night the Titanic
  Sank
Eruption! The Story of Volcanoes
The Story of Columbus
Journey of a Humpback Whale
Amazing Buildings
LEGO: Castle Under Attack
LEGO: Rocket Rescue
¡Insectos! en español
Ice Skating Stars

Level 3

Spacebusters: The Race to the
  Moon
Beastly Tales
Shark Attack!
Titanic
Invaders from Outer Space
Plants Bite Back!
Time Traveler
Bermuda Triangle
Tiger Tales
Zeppelin: The Age of the Airship
Spies
Terror on the Amazon
Disasters at Sea
The Story of Anne Frank

Abraham Lincoln: Lawyer,
  Leader, Legend
George Washington: Soldier,
  Hero, President
Extreme Sports
Spiders' Secrets
LEGO: Mission to the Arctic
NFL: Super Bowl Heroes
MLB: Home Run Heroes: Big
  Mac, Sammy, and Junior
MLB: Roberto Clemente
MLB: World Series Heroes
The Big Dinosaur Dig
Space Heroes: Amazing
  Astronauts

Level 4

Days of the Knights
Volcanoes
Secrets of the Mummies
Pirates: Raiders of the High Seas
Horse Heroes
Micro Monsters
Going for Gold!
Extreme Machines
Flying Ace: The Story of
  Amelia Earhart
Free at Last! The Story of Martin
  Luther King, Jr.
First Flight: The Story of the Wright
  Brothers

The Incredible Hulk's Book of
  Strength
MLB: The Story of the New York
  Yankees
JLA Readers Level 4: Batman's Guide
  to the Universe
JLA Readers Level 4: Superman's
  Guide to the Universe
NFL's Greatest Upsets
NFL: Rumbling Running Backs
LEGO: Race for Survival
NFL: Super Bowl!

A Note to Parents and Teachers

DK READERS is a compelling program for beginning readers, designed in conjunction with leading literacy experts, including Dr. Linda Gambrell, director of the Eugene T. Moore School of Education, Clemson University, and past president of the National Reading Conference.

Beautiful illustrations and superb full-color photographs combine with engaging, easy-to-read stories to offer a fresh approach to each subject in the series. Each DK READER is guaranteed to capture a child's interest while developing his or her reading skills, general knowledge, and love of reading.

The four levels of DK READERS are aimed at different reading abilities, enabling you to choose the books that are exactly right for your child:

Level 1 – Beginning to read
Level 2 — Beginning to read alone
Level 3 — Reading alone
Level 4 — Proficient reader

The "normal" age at which a child begins to read can be anywhere from three to eight years old, so these levels are only a general guideline.

No matter which level you select, you can be sure that you are helping your child learn to read, then read to learn!

LONDON, NEW YORK, TORONTO,
MELBOURNE, MUNICH, and DELHI

Senior Editor Beth Sutinis
Senior Art Editor Michelle Baxter
Publisher Chuck Lang
Creative Director Tina Vaughan
Production Chris Avgherinos

Reading Consultant
Linda Gambrell, Ph.D.

Produced by NFL Creative
Editorial Director John Wiebusch
Managing Editor John Fawaz
Art Director Evelyn Javier

First American Edition, 2003

03 04 05 10 9 8 7 6 5 4 3 2 1
Published in the United States by DK Publishing, Inc.
375 Hudson Street, New York, New York 10014

ISBN: 0-7894-9862-6 (PB)
ISBN: 0-7894-9863-4 (HC)

A Catalog Record is available from the Library of Congress.

Color reproduction by Asia Pacific
Printed and bound in China
by L. Rex Printing Co., Ltd.

Photography credits:
t=top, b=below, l=left, r=right, c=center,
Jennifer L. Abelson cover tc, 6; Sylvia Allen 11; Greg Banner 13;
Scott Boehm 46; Gary Bogdon/*Orlando Sentinel* 29;
Peter Brouillet 9, 15; David Drapkin 3, 20, 26; David
Drapkin/NFLP cover tr, 31; Malcolm Emmons 4;
Michael Hebert 23; Paul Jasienski 16, 25; Allen Kee/NFLP
(inside back cover), 19; Al Messerschmidt 41c, 41b;
Mike Moore 43; Al Pereira 38; JC Ridley/NFLP cover br, 45, 47;
John Sandhaus 5; Bill Smith 48; James D. Smith 32;
Sam Stone 17; Jim Turner cover bl; Jim Turner/NFLP 2, 37;
Courtesy Weber Shandwick Worldwide 35

Discover more at
www.dk.com

Contents

Most Important Position 4

Tom Brady 6

Drew Brees 12

Aaron Brooks 18

Daunte Culpepper 24

Donovan McNabb 30

Chad Pennington 36

Michael Vick 42

Glossary 48

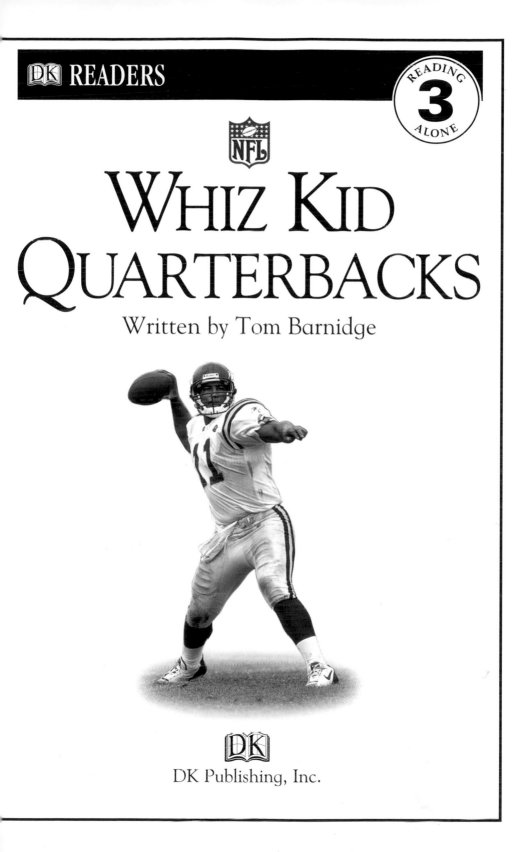

NFL
WHIZ KID
QUARTERBACKS

Written by Tom Barnidge

DK Publishing, Inc.

The Most Important Position

Football is called the ultimate team game. That's because victory depends on all of the players doing their jobs.

But even in the ultimate team game, one player stands above the rest. That is the quarterback, who tells his teammates which plays to run and handles the ball on every offensive play.

He must be skillful with his handoffs, accurate with his passes, and able to avoid being tackled. He often must make split-second decisions.

Two of the best quarterbacks in NFL history were Johnny Unitas and Joe Montana. Unitas led the Baltimore Colts to NFL championships in 1958 and 1959. Montana helped the San Francisco 49ers win four Super Bowls during the 1980s. They were famous for playing their best in the most important games.

Joe Montana

The quarterbacks you will read about in this book are rising NFL stars. Someday, young players may look at them the same way these whiz kids look at Unitas and Montana.

Johnny Unitas was one of the NFL's best.

Tom Brady

When Tom Brady led the New England Patriots to victory in Super Bowl XXXVI, he knew what it was like to live a Cinderella story. At the beginning of the 2001 season, he was a backup quarterback. Five months later, he was the Super Bowl MVP.

Brady has always been a good athlete. In high school, he not only played football but also was an all-star catcher in baseball. The Montreal Expos even drafted him in the 1995 Major League Baseball draft. He decided instead to accept a scholarship to the University of Michigan, where he led his football team to a record of 20–5 in two seasons as a starter.

But Tom wasn't expected to be a star

Almost overnight, Tom Brady became a star.

in the NFL. There were 198 players chosen ahead of him in the 2000 NFL Draft, and, in his rookie season, he was the Patriots' third-string quarterback.

Still…

"There always was something about Tom that made you notice him," center Damien Woody said, "even when he wasn't number one or number two. It was the way he carried himself in the huddle. I know I always said, 'If he could get a chance, it would be interesting to see what he could do.'"

Brady's chance came when starter Drew Bledsoe was injured in week 2 of the 2001 season. Tom led New England to 11 victories in the last 14 games, and then helped them to a playoff victory over Oakland. An injury forced him to leave the AFC title game in Pittsburgh, but Bledsoe stepped in and helped the Patriots win. Suddenly, they were in the Super Bowl.

Some people wondered if Brady would be ready to play. Others wondered if coach Bill

Tom was ready when his chance came.

Belichick would start the veteran Bledsoe. But Belichick said, "Tom Brady is our quarterback." That didn't surprise Brady's college coach.

"Tom Brady is everything you want in a quarterback," Lloyd Carr said. "He's tough-minded and tough physically. The guys really believe in him. And if you knew him, you'd believe in him, too."

Brady faced his biggest challenge at the Super Bowl, when the Patriots and St. Louis Rams were tied 17–17 with just 1 minute 21 seconds to play. Beginning on the Patriots' 17-yard line, he calmly led his team downfield by completing 5 of 8 passes for 53 yards. The clock kept ticking down.

When teammate Adam Vinatieri kicked a 48-yard field goal with no time remaining, the Patriots had won 20–17.

"Super Bowl champions!" Brady screamed on the sideline.

Brady has been the Patriots' quarterback ever since. In 2002, he passed for a league-leading 28 touchdowns, though New England missed the playoffs with a 9–7 record.

The Youngest Winner

Tom Brady became the youngest quarterback to win a Super Bowl when the Patriots defeated the St. Louis Rams in Super Bowl XXXVI on February 3, 2002. On that date, he was 24 years, 184 days old. Until then, Joe Namath and Joe Montana had shared the honor (25 years, 227 days).

Drew Brees

Drew Brees of the San Diego Chargers has been a star athlete for about as long as he has played sports. At Westlake High School in Austin, Texas, he played on both the basketball and baseball teams. But football was the game in which he really shined.

In his two years as the starting quarterback, Brees guided Westlake to a 28–0–1 record. Brees led Westlake to a state championship and was named the Texas Class 5A (big schools) most valuable player in 1996.

He was just as sensational during his college career at Purdue University. He set Big Ten and school records for passing yards (11,792), touchdown passes (90), completion percentage

Drew Brees has been a football star for a long time.

(.611), and total yards (12,693). He led Purdue to the Rose Bowl in 2000, and was named the Big Ten Conference's player of the year in both 1998 and 2000.

Even with all of those accomplishments, Brees was not the first quarterback selected in the 2001 NFL Draft. That honor belonged to Michael Vick. In fact, Brees wasn't drafted until the Chargers took him with the first pick in the second round.

Some NFL scouts thought he was too small (6 feet, 221 pounds). Some thought his arm was not strong enough for pro football. But Brees proved himself when he finally got a chance to play.

In his first season, he was rushed into

The Chargers won as soon as Drew became a starter.

duty against Kansas City when starter Doug Flutie was injured. He rallied his team to a lead after trailing 19–0. In 2002, his second season, he earned the starting quarterback's job and led San Diego to victories in his first four starts. No other Chargers' quarterback ever had done that.

"It's rare that you'll find a quarterback in his first year making as few mistakes as Drew Brees," veteran quarterback Steve Beuerlein said. "He makes plays when he needs to, and he plays the way the coaches ask him to play."

Drew, who was an excellent student in college (he had a 3.40 grade-point average at Purdue), shows his intelligence in the decisions he makes on the field.

"He knows a lot about the game," Broncos coach Mike

At Purdue, Drew was the Big Ten Player of the Year.

Shanahan said, "and he handles himself like a quarterback who knows how to lead and how to win."

In his first full season as a starter, Brees completed 61 percent of his passes for 3,284 yards and 17 touchdowns. He led the Chargers to an 8–8 record—three victories more than 2001—including three wins in overtime.

A Calm Brees

A human being's normal heart rate is 60–70 beats per minute. The number goes up when a person is excited, or if he is out of shape. Drew Brees must be one of the calmest, best-conditioned players in the NFL. When doctors gave him a physical exam before the 2002 season, his heart rate was 38.

Aaron Brooks

Hardly anybody knew of Aaron Brooks when he arrived in the NFL in 1999. He was drafted by Green Bay, which meant he was buried on the Packers' depth chart behind Brett Favre. Even after he was traded to New Orleans, Brooks was overlooked. For the first 11 games of the 2000 season, he was a backup to Jeff Blake.

When Blake was injured, Brooks finally got his chance, and the second-year quarterback quickly proved he was ready to play. Even though he started just five games in 2000, he passed for more than 1,500 yards and 9 touchdowns, and he ran for 2 touchdowns.

He helped the Saints to a 10–6 record and a wild-card playoff victory over the

Aaron Brooks became a star after he joined the Saints.

Aaron, who is tall and quick, is also an excellent passer.

St. Louis Rams. It was the first playoff victory in Saints franchise history.

"I knew he was going to be a premier player in this league," Favre said. "All he needed was the opportunity."

Brooks got his opportunity because of Mike McCarthy, who had been the Packers' quarterbacks coach when Brooks was a rookie. When McCarthy joined the Saints as offensive coordinator in 2000, he suggested to the Saints that they trade for Aaron.

"When you work with someone every day, you have a better understanding of their abilities," McCarthy said.

Brooks, who is lanky (6 feet 4 inches) and quick, has the ability to avoid tacklers and to pass while on the run. He demonstrated those skills at the

University of Virginia, where he earned a degree in anthropology. On the field, he set a school record with six career 300-yard passing games, and he ran for 13 touchdowns.

What's different in the NFL?

"The speed and tempo of the game," Brooks said. "You are playing against the best athletes in the world."

In 2001, his first full season as a starter, he passed for 3,832 yards and 26 touchdowns. But because he also threw 22 interceptions, and the Saints slumped to 7–9, Brooks worked hard in the offseason to improve his performance.

In 2002, even though he was troubled with nagging injuries, Brooks passed for more touchdowns (27) and fewer interceptions (15). He helped the Saints to another winning (9–7) season. Two of their victories came against the Tampa Bay Buccaneers, the eventual Super Bowl champions.

"Aaron has done everything we asked," McCarthy said. "He's everything I thought he would be."

Quarterback Cousins

Aaron Brooks isn't the only star quarterback in his family. Quarterback Michael Vick (7) of the Atlanta Falcons is his second cousin. They both grew up in Newport News, Virginia, although they went to different high schools. Aaron attended Homer L. Ferguson. Michael went to Warwick. Brooks, 27, is four years older than his cousin.

Daunte Culpepper

Five quarterbacks were selected in the
first round of the 1999 NFL Draft, but it
is easy to tell Daunte Culpepper from
the rest. At 6 feet 4 inches and 255
pounds, he easily is the biggest
quarterback in the game.

But it's not just Daunte's size that sets
him apart. It's all the other things about
him—his speed, his strength, his athletic
ability, and the unpredictable way he
plays his position. Culpepper can
outmuscle defenders, run over tacklers,
or outrace them downfield. He can make
time for a receiver to get open by
scrambling around in the backfield.

He has been timed at 4.6 seconds for
the 40-yard dash—a time normally
associated with a running back. He has

Everything about Daunte Culpepper is big—even his smile.

a vertical leap of 36 inches—the kind of jumping ability usually seen in a wide receiver. He can bench press 345 pounds. And he can throw a football more than 70 yards—about the same as Packers superstar Brett Favre.

"You're not going to find many quarterbacks that have his combination of size, speed, and the accuracy as a passer," said defensive end Grant Wistrom of the St. Louis Rams.

Daunte caught scouts' attention when he starred at Central Florida University, where he set more than 30 school records. He also holds the NCAA record for completion percentage in a single season. Daunte's percentage of 73.6 in 1998 meant he completed almost 3 out of every 4 passes he attempted. Culpepper broke a record set 15 years earlier by Steve Young at Brigham Young.

Still, NFL success didn't come overnight. Culpepper, who was drafted by the Minnesota Vikings, spent his rookie season as the number-three quarterback behind Jeff George and

Daunte is stronger and faster than most quarterbacks.

Randall Cunningham. He appeared in only one game and did not attempt a pass. So fans and reporters were surprised in 2000 when coach Dennis Green announced that Culpepper would be his starting quarterback.

Daunte was a quick learner. He proved that he was ready for the job by leading the Vikings to victories in their first seven games. The team finished with an 11–5 record, won the NFC Central Division title, and advanced to the NFC Championship Game. Daunte passed for 3,937 yards and 33 touchdowns in 2000, and he was selected to play in the Pro Bowl, the NFL's all-star game.

Knee injuries bothered Daunte in 2001, forcing him to miss five games. In

2002, the Vikings had a new coach, Mike Tice, and they struggled in their early games. But by the end of the season, Culpepper was back on track. He passed for 18 touchdowns, and he ran for 10 more. Minnesota fans are expecting more big things from their big quarterback.

Daunte's Angel

Daunte Culpepper refers to his adoptive mother, Emma Culpepper, as his "angel" because she was there when he needed her. Emma was 62 years old when she took in the 1-day-old infant who was up for adoption. "She is a very, very special lady," Daunte says. "She is the person who made me the person I am today."

Donovan McNabb

Philadelphia fans booed on draft day in 1999, when the Eagles used their first pick to choose quarterback Donovan McNabb from Syracuse University. Eagles fans wanted their team to pick running back Ricky Williams, who led the nation in rushing at the University of Texas.

"I didn't take it personally," said McNabb, "but it was embarrassing for my mom and dad."

Since then, McNabb has changed jeers to cheers by leading the Eagles to three playoff berths and two appearances in the NFC Championship Game. He was chosen three times for the Pro Bowl and set a club record for pass completions (330) in 2000. In just four

Donovan McNabb has turned jeers to cheers.

Donovan is like "a coach on the field," his coach says.

seasons, he has passed for 9,835 yards and 71 touchdowns while throwing only 38 interceptions. He also has run for 1,884 yards and 14 touchdowns.

"Donovan is not only a great football player, he's a great leader," Eagles coach Andy Reid said. "It's like I have a coach on the field."

McNabb is more than just a good passer. He is good at avoiding the pass rush, and he can take off and run with the ball. At 6 feet 3 inches and 226 pounds, he is difficult to tackle, and he is remarkably fast.

McNabb didn't make an immediate impact in the NFL. In his first season, he was a backup for the first nine games. Then he replaced Doug Pederson, he was sacked 13 times and threw 4 interceptions in five starts. The Eagles won only one of those games.

"I started out pretty shaky," he said. "With the help of my teammates and the people in the organization, we were able to stay focused."

McNabb has the perfect attitude for his job. He is not easily upset, and he has a great sense of humor. His teammates talk about how playful he can be in tense situations.

"Donovan is like [Green Bay quarterback] Brett Favre," said Reid, who was an assistant coach for the Packers. "Both can be the funniest guy on the bus, but the most serious on the field when it's time to be."

McNabb was sensational in 2002. He threw 17 touchdown passes and only 6 interceptions in the first 10 games, but his season was cut short because of a broken ankle. Donovan was healthy in time for the playoffs, and Philadelphia fans cheered his return. That was a lot different from the way he was greeted four years earlier.

McNabb's Biggest Fan

When the people at Campbell's Chunky Soup looked for football stars and their mothers to appear in commercials, it was no surprise that they picked Donovan McNabb. Donovan and his mom, Wilma, are about as close as a mother and son can be. "Mom is my number-one fan," Donovan said, "and she's also my number-one critic."

Chad Pennington

Chad had to bide his time before tasting success in the NFL. Although he was selected in the first round of the 2000 draft, he spent his rookie season as the New York Jets' third-string quarterback. He was a backup again in 2001, attempting only 20 passes and playing in only two games.

The 2002 season started out the same way. But when starter Vinny Testaverde struggled in the first four games, Pennington came in and made the most of his chance. He set a club record for completion percentage (68.9) and passed for 3,120 yards. He completed 22 touchdown passes and led the NFL in passer rating (104.2).

More importantly, he helped the Jets

Chad Pennington led the NFL in passer rating in 2002.

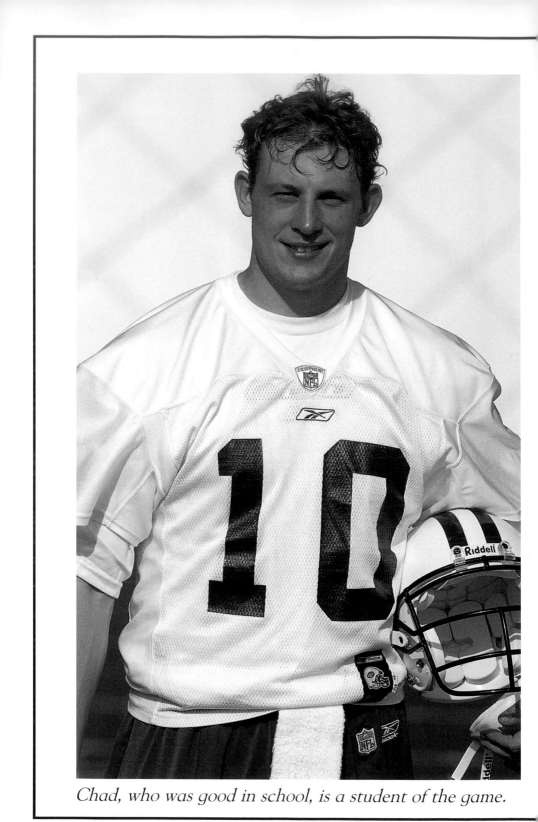

Chad, who was good in school, is a student of the game.

overcome a 1–4 start to post a 9–7 record and win the AFC East title.

"He proved himself," said teammate Kevin Mawae. "He showed a lot of poise and confidence."

Pennington's biggest asset is his intelligence. At Marshall University, where he majored in journalism, he had a 3.8 grade-point average. As a senior, he was selected by the St. Louis Athletic Club as the top student-athlete in the country, and he was a finalist for a Rhodes Scholarship.

"We're all here because of our physical abilities," Chad said, "but the ability to stay in this league depends on your mental capabilities and how you handle situations."

Pennington does not have a strong

throwing arm, but he is extremely accurate with his passes. He is not particularly nifty on his feet, but he is good at reading blitzes and analyzing pass coverages.

Jets offensive coordinator Paul Hackett said he was impressed by Pennington's ability to come in and immediately run the offense.

"He's in total control of what's going on," Hackett said.

One of his best games came in a 30–17 victory over the New England Patriots in week 16. With the score tied 17–17 in the third quarter, Pennington led the Jets on three successive scoring drives. He finished with 285 passing yards and 3 touchdowns.

Pennington's teammates weren't

surprised at his clutch performance.

"Over the past couple of years, when he was waiting for his chance, I saw him prepare like no one I've ever seen before," wide receiver Laveranues Coles said. "He's just a special player. He's a smart guy. He's a student of the game, and that's hard to come by."

Some Combination

One of the first receivers to appreciate Chad Pennington was Minnesota Vikings star Randy Moss. They were teammates at Marshall University. In 1997, they set an NCAA record for touchdown passes (24) by a quarterback-receiver duo. "Chad's not the most mobile quarterback," Moss said, "but as far as his reads and his approach, he's with it."

Michael Vick

The Atlanta Falcons were so eager to select Michael in the 2001 NFL Draft that they agreed to trade three draft choices and wide receiver Tim Dwight to the San Diego Chargers for the number-one pick.

Vick gave a hint of his talent in two years at Virginia Tech. As a runner, he had blinding speed. As a passer, he set four school records. As a starting quarterback, he led his team to a 20–1 record. He was almost a one-man show.

The only question was how quickly he could adjust to life in the NFL, where game plans are more complex and the competition is more talented. In pro football, one-man shows don't usually work.

Michael Vick was at the top of the Falcons' shopping list.

Michael spent most of his rookie season as a backup to Chris Chandler. When he played—he appeared in eight games—he was sometimes great, sometimes disappointing.

"I'd always come in and start off good," he said, "and then there'd be something that set me back. It would be a fumble or a sack. We'd get in a third-and-long situation. That would change the whole game."

But even opponents could see Michael's potential.

"He's the fastest guy I've seen in my whole life," the St. Louis Rams' Leonard Little said.

"He's the best athlete in the NFL," said Miami Dolphins cornerback Patrick Surtain.

The 2002 season was Michael's coming-out party. He was the Falcons' starting quarterback, and he shined in the role. He passed for 2,936 yards and he ran for 777. He passed for 16 touchdowns, and he scored 8. He led the Falcons to a 9–6–1 record and their first playoff berth in four years.

During the season, he showed off the skills that set him apart. He dodged, darted,

changed
direction,
and
frustrated
defenders
throughout the league.
Sometimes, he passed. Sometimes, he ran. Opponents never could anticipate what he would do next.

"He's elusive, he has a great arm, and he's fast," said New York Giants defensive end Michael Strahan. "He's going to be a quarterback in this league for a long time."

One of Vick's most memorable performances came against the Minnesota Vikings. He didn't pass well—only 11 completions for 173 yards—but, oh, how he ran. He carried

10 times for 173 yards—the most ever by a quarterback—and finished with a dazzling 46-yard touchdown run in overtime that gave Atlanta a thrilling 30–24 victory.

Said Falcons coach Dan Reeves, "I've never seen anyone turn on the jets like that."

Lucky Number 7

Michael Vick needed a full year before he felt comfortable in the NFL. Fans didn't need that long to know that they liked the way he played. Michael's number 7 jersey was the sixth-best seller among all the player jerseys on sale at NFLShop.com the first year it was offered. He was the only rookie to rank among the top 10.

Glossary

AFC
The American Football Conference, consisting of 16 of the NFL's 32 teams.

Bench Press
A weightlifting exercise done while reclining on a bench.

Center
An offensive lineman who hikes the football to the quarterback.

Completion
A forward pass that is thrown and caught by the offense.

Fumble
Loss of possession of the football by a ball carrier.

Handoff
The act of transferring the ball from one player to another.

Huddle
A gathering of players in which they discuss strategy.

Interception
A pass intended for an offensive player that is caught by a defender.

NFC
The National Football Conference, consisting of 16 of the NFL's 32 teams.

NFL Draft
The annual selection of college players by NFL teams.

Offensive Coordinator
An assistant coach who is in charge of the offense.

Pass Rush
An effort to tackle the quarterback before he can throw a pass.

Playoffs
Games played after the regular season to determine the league champion.

Rookie
A player in his first season.

Sack
Tackling a quarterback before he is able to pass.

Snap
The act of hiking the ball to the quarterback.

Vertical Leap
The measurement of a player's ability to jump straight up.

Index

Atlanta Falcons 23, 42, 43, 45, 47

Baltimore Colts 5
Belichick, Bill 9
Beuerlein, Steve 16
Blake, Jeff 18
Bledsoe, Drew 8-10
Brady, Tom 6-11
Brees, Drew 12-17
Brigham Young University 27
Brooks, Aaron 18-23

Campbell's Chunky Soup 35
Carr, Lloyd 10
Chandler, Chris 44
Coles, Laveranues 41
Culpepper, Daunte 24-29
Culpepper, Emma 29
Cunningham, Randall 28

Dwight, Tim 42

Favre, Brett 18, 26, 34
Flutie, Doug 15

George, Jeff 27
Green Bay Packers 18

Hackett, Paul 40

Little, Leonard 44

Marshall University 39, 41
Mawae, Kevin 39

McCarthy, Mike 21
McNabb, Donovan 30-35
McNabb, Wilma 35
Michigan, University of 6
Minnesota Vikings 27-29, 46
Montana, Joe 5, 11
Montreal Expos 6
Moss, Randy 41

Namath, Joe 11
New England Patriots 6, 8-11, 40
New Orleans Saints 18-19, 21-22
New York Jets 36, 40

Pederson, Doug 33
Pennington, Chad 36-41
Philadelphia Eagles 30, 33-34
Pro Bowl 28, 30
Purdue University 16

Reeves, Dan 47
Reid, Andy 33-34
Rhodes Scholarship 39

St. Louis Athletic Club 39
St. Louis Rams 10-11
San Diego Chargers 12, 14-15, 17
San Francisco 49ers 5
Shanahan, Mike 16
Strahan, Michael 46

Super Bowl XXXVI 6
Surtain, Patrick 44
Syracuse University 30

Tampa Bay Buccaneers 23
Testaverde, Vinny 36
Texas, University of 30
Tice, Mike 29

Unitas, Johnny 5

Vick, Michael 14, 23, 42-47
Vinatieri, Adam 10
Virginia, University of 22
Virginia Tech 42

Westlake High School 12
Williams, Ricky 30
Wistrom, Grant 27
Woody, Damien 8

Young, Steve 27